Simply Science

BODY AND HEALTH

Discover Science Through Facts and Fun

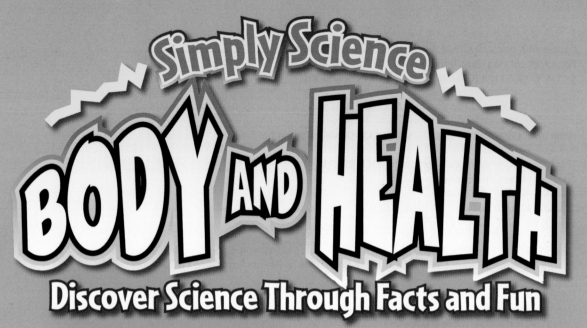

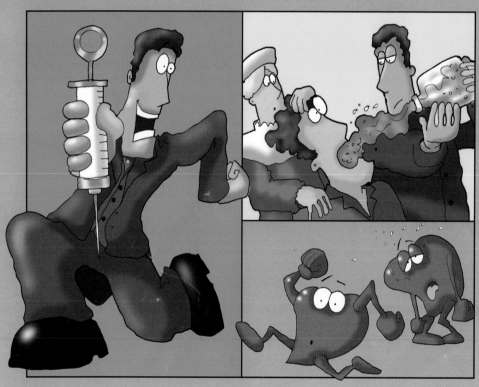

By Gerry Bailey and Steve Way

Science and curriculum consultant:

Debra Voege, M.A., science curriculum resource teacher

Gareth Stevens
Publishing

Please visit our web site at www.garethstevens.com.
For a free catalog describing our list of high-quality books, call 1-800-542-2595 (USA)
or 1-800-387-3178 (Canada). Our fax: 1-877-542-2596

Library of Congress Cataloging-in-Publication Data available upon request from publisher.

ISBN-10: 1-4339-0030-0   ISBN-13: 978-1-4339-0030-3 (lib. bdg.)

This North American edition first published in 2009 by
Gareth Stevens Publishing
A Weekly Reader® Company
1 Reader's Digest Road
Pleasantville, NY 10570-7000 USA

This U.S. edition copyright © 2009 by Gareth Stevens, Inc. Original edition copyright © 2008 by
Allegra Publishing, First published in Great Britain in 2008 by Allegra Publishing Ltd, London.

Gareth Stevens Executive Managing Editor: Lisa M. Herrington
Gareth Stevens Creative Director: Lisa Donovan
Gareth Stevens Designer: Keith Plechaty
Gareth Stevens Associate Editor: Amanda Hudson
Gareth Stevens Publisher: Keith Garton
Special thanks to Jessica Cohn

Photo Credits: Cover (tc) Javier/Shutterstock Inc., (bl) Eric Gevaert/Shutterstock Inc.; p. 5 Ariel Skelley/CORBIS; p. 9
Javier/Shutterstock Inc.; p. 12 Stanislav Komogorov/Shutterstock Inc.; p. 13 Eric Gevaert/Shutterstock Inc.; p. 21 H. G.
Rossi/zefa/CORBIS.; pp. 22-23 Steve Satushek/Photographers Choice/Getty Images; p. 25 (t) Jose Fuente/Shutterstock
Inc., p. 25 (b) Doug Scott, Chris Bonington Picture Library.

Illustrations: Steve Boulter and Xact Studio

Diagrams: Karen Radford

Printed in the United States of America

1 2 3 4 5 6 7 8 9 13 12 11 10 09 08

CONTENTS

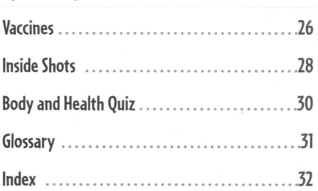

Working Parts

You certainly know what your body is. But do you know how your body works? It runs like the most complicated and clever machine ever built!

Like any machine with working parts, your body needs special care. It needs healthful food and plenty of exercise to stay strong. If something goes wrong with your body, you can work to make it right again. When you take care of your body, it takes care of you!

Your body works with...
your bones...
    your muscles...
and your clever brain!

Your body works to
stay healthy and fit!

Exercise helps to keep your body fit.

Your Bony Frame

Your bones—all 206 of them—link together to form your skeleton. This bony frame is what holds you up. The bones also protect important parts of your body. Your skeleton shelters the heart, lungs, and other organs inside of you.

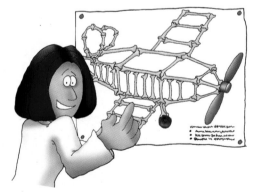

Bones are good at their jobs. Most bones are stronger and lighter than aluminium—the metal used to make airplane frames.

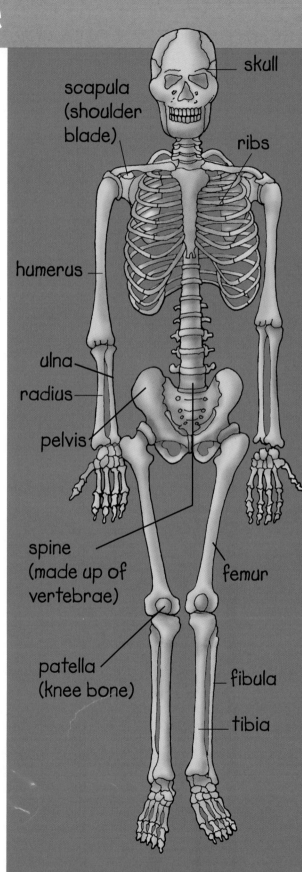

scapula (shoulder blade)

skull

ribs

humerus

ulna

radius

pelvis

spine (made up of vertebrae)

femur

patella (knee bone)

fibula

tibia

Keeping Things Moving

Big bones give your muscles something to pull on or pull against. These bones stay in place but allow you to move your body.

Tiny bones in the middle of your ears carry sound to the skull so you can hear. Your smallest bone is in your ear. Bones of all sizes help keep things moving.

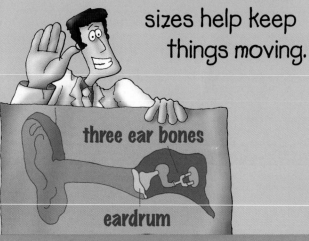

three ear bones

eardrum

Keeping Things Safe

Because they are strong, bones protect important parts of the body. The skull protects the brain. The spine shields nerves that link to your brain, sending messages all around your body. Your hard rib cage protects your lungs and heart.

Making Blood

Your bones aren't hollow. They are filled with **bone marrow**. One type of bone marrow stores fat from your diet. Another type helps make red blood cells, which carry oxygen around the body, as well as white blood cells, which help fight off disease.

Seeing Inside

1. Gases are matter that is neither solid nor liquid. Wilhelm Roentgen, a scientist, set up a lab to study gases. His experiments were a bit dangerous!

2. He tried to see what happened when an electric current passed through a tube of gas. Would it get hot, or perhaps light up?

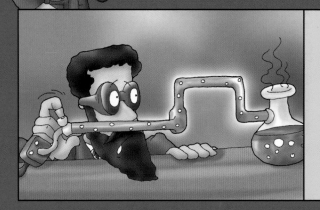

3. He noticed a strange thing. When the current was on, certain chemicals in the lab started to glow! When the electricity was off, the glow switched off. So something was coming from the tube. It was some kind of ray!

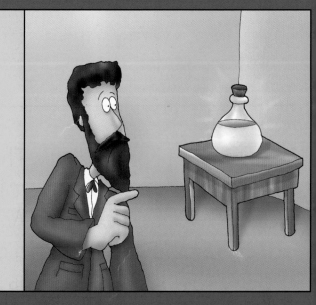

X-Ray Pictures

Doctors use invisible rays of energy to take pictures of your bones. These rays are called X-rays. The machines that send out the rays work like cameras.

4. He studied the ray. He found that the ray could pass through soft objects but not hard ones.

5. Roentgen called the ray an **X-ray**. He built a machine that fired X-rays at a steel plate. When he held his hand in front of it, the rays passed through everything except his bones. The bones showed up as dark areas on the plate.

X-rays are invisible light waves known as radiation. Radiation can pass through soft objects. X-rays can pass through your skin, and you don't even feel them! Radiation does not pass through hard objects. On film, the rays show objects that absorb them. So your bones show up as light areas on X-rays.

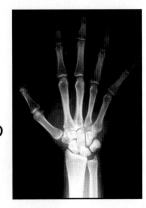

Body Pump

Your heart and blood are part of the same circulatory system within the body. Your hard-working heart pumps blood throughout your body.

Measuring blood pressure shows how well the heart and arteries are working.

What Is Blood Made Of?

Your blood is one color: reddish. Yet it's made of a mixture of hundreds of things. The most important of these blood parts are:

 plasma

 red blood cells

 white blood cells

 platelets

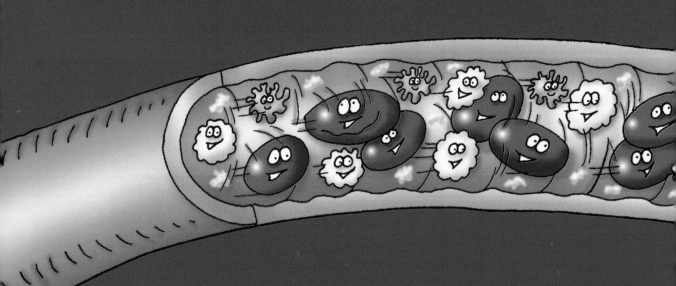

Red Blood Cells

Why is blood reddish? Most of the cells in your blood are **red blood cells**. They contain a chemical that makes them bright red. These red blood cells have a very important job. They grab oxygen as your blood goes through your lungs. Red cells carry the oxygen through tubes, called arteries, to every part of your body.

Platelets

Platelets are cell particles that help your blood clot when you get a cut. Clots stop the bleeding and form scabs to protect the wound.

Plasma

The light yellow liquid part of the blood is made mainly of water. It can pass out of the blood and fill body cells. There are many chemicals in this special water that the body needs.

White Blood Cells

Some **white blood cells** help fight invading cells that can make you ill. The white cells catch these "bugs" and kill them with deadly chemicals. Other white cells make antibodies and anti-toxins. These chemicals kill the bugs or clean up the damage the bugs make inside you.

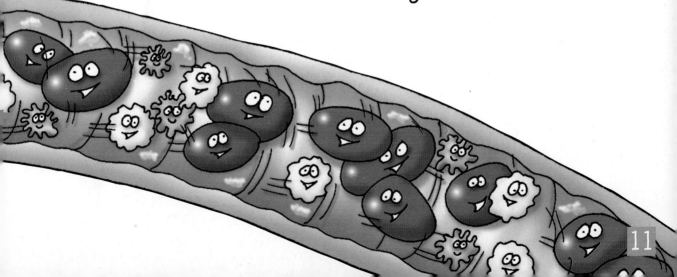

Your Muscles

Weightlifters have plenty of power. You can tell by the size of their muscles. Muscles make us strong and do many other jobs, too.

Most of your muscles are attached to the bones of your skeleton. The attached muscles are known as **skeletal muscles**.

Your muscles work in pairs to allow you to make movements. When you lift your hand toward your face, a muscle in the upper arm, called the bicep, pulls a bone in the lower arm upward. Then, when you want to lower your hand, a muscle at the back of the upper arm, called the tricep, pulls another bone in the lower arm downward.

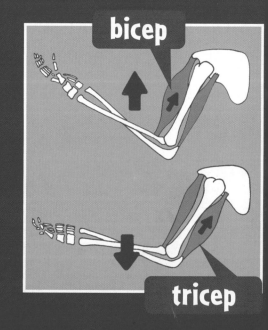

bicep

tricep

Smooth Muscles

A second type of muscle is known as smooth muscle. That is a good name for it! **Smooth muscle** helps food move smoothly through your digestive system. It also helps blood flow smoothly through your arteries and veins.

Cardiac Muscle

Cardiac muscle is found only in the heart. This one-of-a-kind muscle keeps your heart beating. This muscle never gets tired, which is a very good way for heart muscle to be!

Twitching Muscles

You also have "slow twitch" muscles, which allow you to keep doing something for a long time. A long-distance runner builds up his or her slow twitch muscles.

"Fast twitch" muscles allow you to carry out intense activity. A sprinter builds up his or her fast twitch muscles.

Hearing, Seeing, Smelling

Our ears allow us to hear sound. Our eyes give us the ability to see. Our noses let us smell things. These organs are responsible for hearing, smelling, and seeing, which are three of our senses. The organs send messages to our brains so we can sense what's going on.

Hearing

Your ears pick up sound. Sound is made of waves that make parts of the ear move. The movement signals the brain. The brain tells you what you hear.

Your Ears

Apart from the part of your ears that you can see, your skull protects your ears. You need to do your part to protect your ears from loud sounds, though. As well as helping you hear, ears help you balance properly. Having two ears helps you work out the source of sounds.

Seeing

Seeing may be the most important sense. More of your brain deals with seeing than with any of the other senses.

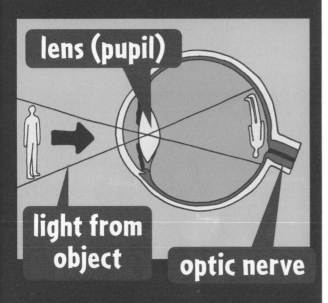

lens (pupil)

light from object

optic nerve

Your eyes each contain a **lens** that lets in light. This lens works like a camera to show what you see. Light makes an upside-down picture on the back of the eye. Nerves carry the picture to the brain. The brain tells you what's there, right side up!

Smelling

You use your nose to breathe through and to smell things. Receptors pick up smells and send a message to your brain. The brain tells you what you're smelling.

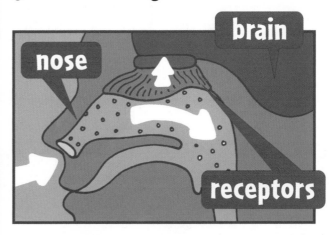

brain

nose

receptors

Eyes on You

Spectacles are frames that hold lenses in front of the eyes. "Specs" can help people see more clearly.

The first spectacles were probably made in Italy around 1280. Some historians think the Chinese invented them long before that, however.

I can see clearly now!

Seeing With Spectacles

1. Scribes, who copied manuscripts day after day, often developed bad eyesight.

2. Then someone came across a lens-shaped piece of glass that bulged in the middle.

Lenses

The lenses of spectacles are **concave** or **convex**. Concave means they curve inward. Concave lenses help people see things far away. Convex lenses bulge outward. They're for people who have problems seeing things close up.

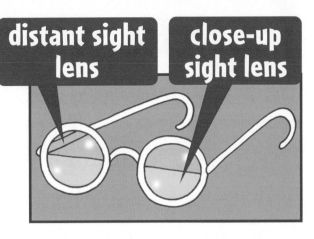

distant sight lens

close-up sight lens

Some lenses are split into two parts, one for close-up sight and one for distance.

3. Looking through the glass made words larger and clearer.

4. You had to hold the lens to use it, though. That was like having extra work. Then came spectacles!

5. Spectacles are still helping people. A frame holds the lenses and balances on the nose. The frame holds two lenses, so there is one to help each eye see better.

17

Tooth Repair

We know we must look after our teeth, or they will rot and fall out. Long ago, however, people were not as careful. Many people lost their teeth when they were quite young. They had to use false teeth instead.

A Mouthful of Teeth

1. In early times, teeth couldn't be replaced. They just fell out, leaving gaps in the mouth.

2. The first dentists weren't very skilled. As time went on, dentists learned to fasten a false tooth to existing teeth. They used a bridge, a kind of wire clip. Early false teeth were made of gold, however, so only wealthy people had them.

Plastics to the Rescue

False teeth are usually fixed to a plate, or **denture**, which fits into the mouth. Plastic is an artificial material that can be formed into lightweight and washable shapes. It works well for teeth. Plastics are made up of long chains of molecules called polymers. It is easy to shape this material when it is hot.

3. Dentists needed a cheaper bridge—something that could be fitted into the mouth and make contact with every part of the gum to hold it secure. The bridge also had to be light and washable. Plastic was the answer.

4. Plastic dentures have helped many people. A plastic mold is shaped to fit the mouth while the plastic is soft. Once it hardens, the mold is filled with a gum-colored base. The teeth are fitted in position. A kind of glue keeps the mold in place.

Stopping Pain

1. The first surgeons operated without anything to help deaden the pain. They could only deaden the patient!

2. On many occasions, operations caused more shock and pain than the injury.

3. In 1800, chemist Sir Humphrey Davy suggested that breathing nitrous oxide could kill feeling in the body. The new idea didn't get much notice.

4. Almost half a century later, Horace Wells used nitrous oxide on himself before he had a tooth pulled out.

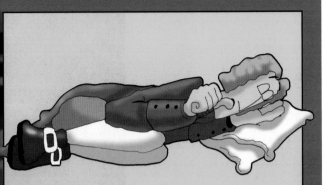

5. Around the same time, a doctor known as Dr. Long had a patient breathe ether to deaden pain. Credit for first using a pain killer, or anesthetic, has been given to William Morton, however. He was a Boston dentist who had many patients breathe ether before he pulled their teeth. We can be grateful to Dr. Morton for making our trips to the dentist a lot more pleasant!

Doctors who specialize in anesthetics are called anesthesiologists. ▶

Anesthetics

An **anesthetic** is a drug that makes people lose sensation, or feeling, in all or part of the body. The loss of feeling is called anesthesia.

A general anesthetic causes you to lose feeling in every part of your body. A local anesthetic makes you lose feeling only in the part that's going to be operated on.

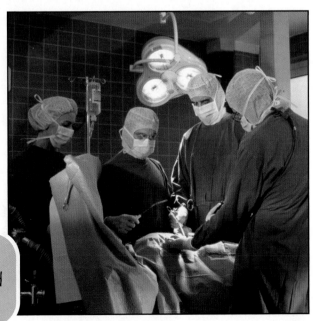

Food for Energy

Besides air and water, we need food to stay alive. Food is the fuel that gives us energy. We need energy to keep our hearts beating and to do all the other things we do. We even need food for thinking!

Food

Food fuels our bodies just like gasoline fuels a car. When food passes into the stomach, it starts to be broken down. The good bits are used, and the rest is pushed out. Chemicals in the food send energy into the cells of the body. This helps us to move and grow. It also helps the body repair cells that have been injured or damaged.

Colorful foods are often the most healthy.

Open Airways

Like most living things, humans need **oxygen** to stay alive. Oxygen can pass through the surface of plants. The surface of humans is skin, and skin is too thick to let oxygen pass! We have to breathe oxygen with our lungs.

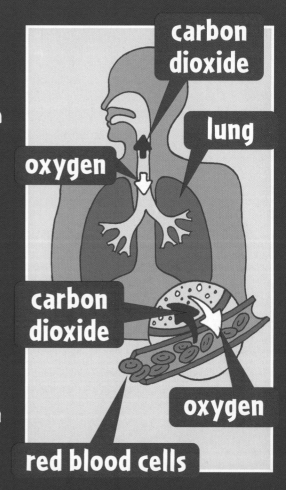

Oxygen

When we breathe in, we take in oxygen. Our cells need oxygen. In our lungs, oxygen passes through thin lung skin, passing into red blood cells. The red cells flow in the blood, which carries oxygen to cells throughout the body.

Carbon Dioxide

At the same time, waste gas that is mostly carbon dioxide passes from the blood and back into the lungs. We get rid of this gas when we breathe out.

carbon dioxide

lung

oxygen

carbon dioxide

oxygen

red blood cells

Thin Air

As you rise higher and higher above the surface of the ground, the air gets thinner. There is less oxygen. People who live in high mountains develop thicker blood that can carry more oxygen. When climbing Mount Everest, the tallest mountain in the world, most climbers carry oxygen cans so they can breathe.

A climber breathes in oxygen through a mask.

Vaccines

A **vaccination** is a dose of medicine that can help protect you from an illness. The dose contains some of the germs which cause the disease. How does that work?

A vaccine causes the body's immune system to attack the germs. The immune system is a natural defense mechanism that seeks out germs and destroys them.

The immune system is tricked into taking action against the small number of germs in the vaccine. The system sets up a permanent defense in case that type of germ attacks the body again.

1. Not long ago, smallpox disease often made people blind or even killed them. Many horrible diseases were quite common then.

2. Doctors knew that smallpox spread easily. They also knew that people did not seem to get smallpox more than once. Then Dr. Edward Jenner noticed something even more important. Dairy workers who caught cowpox, a mild disease like smallpox, never caught it again. The workers did not get smallpox, either.

Germs That Protect Against Disease

3. He wonderered if a small dose of the cowpox germs might build resistance to smallpox in a patient. He knew that proving his idea would be risky. What if the idea did not work?

5. James caught cowpox. When he recovered, Jenner injected him with smallpox pus. They waited and waited.

6. James did not catch smallpox. The injection worked! It stopped James from catching smallpox. Soon the new vaccine was used to cure and prevent smallpox. Perhaps the biggest hero was James.

4. James Phipps was the son of Jenner's gardener. With permission, Jenner took pus from a dairymaid with cowpox. He injected it into cuts in the boy's hand.

Inside Shots

Before shots, more people died from illness than do now. Shots are syringes, tubes with plungers at the top and hollow needles below. A doctor sticks a needle in a patient's skin and pumps medicine in the hollow. The body does the rest of the work!

> We find new medicines all the time.

A Pump to Give Medicine

1. When patients eat or drink medicine, it takes a while for the body to absorb the medicine. In some cases, it can take too long to be helpful.

2. Doctors had to find ways to get medicine into the bloodstream faster. One of the first things they tried was spreading medicine onto wounds.

A Syringe Is a Pump

A pump has a piston that moves in and out of a cylinder. As the piston moves one way, it pulls liquid or gas into the cylinder. When it moves the other way, it pushes liquid or gas out. In a syringe, the piston is the plunger. The cylinder is the tube. The liquid is medicine!

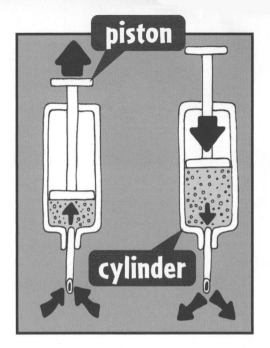

3. They pricked the skin with a needle and poured medicine through the tiny wound.

4. Then Francis Rynd invented a needle that could inject medicine under the skin. The medicine went into a blood vein. It passed into the body fast!

5. The needle he used was hollow. That way, medicine could be pumped through it.

6. He fixed the needle to a cylinder with a piston at the top. This helped him control the speed at which medicine was given.

Body and Health Quiz

1. In which part of the body would you find the smallest bone?

2. What special type of muscle is found in the heart?

3. How many bones are in the human body?

4. What is the name for a drug that makes people lose feeling?

5. What color are the blood cells that help people fight disease?

6. What shape lenses help people read?

7. What material is usually used to make false teeth?

8. What are the three main parts of a syringe?

9. What gas did Sir Humphrey Davy suggest as an anesthetic in 1800?

10. What fuel gives humans energy?

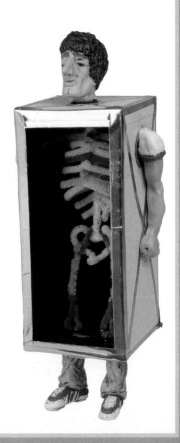

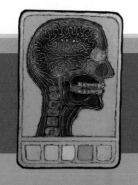

1. Ear 2. Cardiac muscle 3. 206 4. An anesthetic 5. White 6. Convex lenses 7. Plastic 8. A tube with a plunger and a needle 9. Nitrous oxide 10. Food

Glossary

anesthetic: a drug that makes people lose sensation, useful for blocking pain

bone marrow: an important material inside bone that creates blood cells

carbon dioxide: a gas that the body pumps out as waste

cardiac muscle: specialized tissue that helps keep the heart pumping

concave lens: lens that curves inward, used to help people see far-off objects

convex lens: lens that curves outward, used to help people see nearby objects

denture: a small plate that fits inside the mouth, securing false teeth

lens: a part of the eye, also known as the pupil, which lets in light

optic nerve: a nerve leading to and from the back of the eye

oxygen: a chemical element that humans and other living things need

plasma: light yellow liquid blood part filled with chemicals a body needs

platelets: cell particles that help blood clot when a person suffers a wound

red blood cells: particles in blood that carry oxygen throughout the body

skeletal muscles: tissues that are attached to and help move and protect bone

smooth muscle: tissue that helps blood flow and food move through a body

vaccination: dose of medicine delivered through a shot, or syringe

white blood cells: particles in blood that help fight and rid a body of disease

X-ray: an invisible light wave used to help photograph the skeleton

Index